GERMAN U-BOAT ACE

Adalbert Schnee

GERMAN U-BOAT ACE
Luc Braeuer

Adalbert Schnee

The Patrols of U-201 in World War II

Schiffer Publishing Ltd

4880 Lower Valley Road • Atglen, PA 19310

The author would like to thank the people who helped him write this book; mainly Mr. Horst Bredow, creator of the U-boat Archives in Cuxhaven, Mrs. Inge Schnee, the Michelsen family, Mr. Jacques Alaluquetas, and Mr. Alain Durrieu for his proof reading.

Library of Congress Control Number: 2015932634

Originally published as, *U-Boote Adalbert Schnee, L'as du U-201*, by Zéphyr BD, Paris, France © 2012. Translated from the French by Omicron Language Solutions, LLC.

Type set in Agency FB/Minion Pro

ISBN: 978-0-7643-4823-5
Printed in China

Published by Schiffer Publishing, Ltd.
4880 Lower Valley Road
Atglen, PA 19310
Phone: (610) 593-1777; Fax: (610) 593-2002
E-mail: Info@schifferbooks.com

For our complete selection of fine books on this and related subjects,
please visit our website at www.schifferbooks.com. You may also write for a free catalog.

This book may be purchased from the publisher. Please try your bookstore first.

We are always looking for people to write books on new and related subjects.
If you have an idea for a book, please contact us at proposals@schifferbooks.com.

Schiffer Publishing's titles are available at special discounts for bulk purchases for sales promotions or premiums. Special editions, including personalized covers, corporate imprints, and excerpts can be created in large quantities for special needs. For more information, contact the publisher.

CONTENTS

Biographies written about German U-boat commanders are very rare, and until now, none have been written about Adalbert Schnee. However, he is one of the few commanders who symbolize the evolution of the German U-boat corps during the Second World War.

"Adi" Schnee was second-in-command under Otto Kretschmer on U-23 from October 1937 to December 1939 and together they carried out five combat patrols, which earned him the Iron Cross 2nd Class. In 1940, Adalbert Schnee successively commanded the three II-type U-boats, U-6, U-60 and U-121, with which he chalked up his first success in the Atlantic and won the Iron Cross 1st Class.

At the beginning of 1941, he was given the command of U-201, the first VIIC-type U-boat affected to the 1st Flotilla; within eighteen months, during the seven patrols with this U-Boat which took him right to the American and African coastlines, he won the highest Wehrmacht decoration of the war: The Knight's Cross with Oak Leaves.

With fifteen ships sunk among the convoys in the middle of the Atlantic, he became a specialist in the style of attack approved by Admiral Dönitz. After this, he joined the General Staff of the U-boat corps and for eighteen months gave them the benefit of his experience, becoming a specialist in the fight against Allied convoys.

In July 1944, he was appointed to supervise the last stages of the construction of his future U-boat, a revolutionary XXI-type. With U-2511, he travelled to Norway where in 1945 he was the only commander to carry out a combat patrol with an XXI.

Thanks to contacts with his family members and with help from his U-boat logbooks preserved in the Cuxhaven U-boat Archives, we can take you through the training and combat engagement of Adi Schnee, the convoy specialist. Finally, the recent discovery of negatives owned by war correspondent Prokop, who took part in a patrol aboard U-201, allows us to illustrate his career.

Adalbert Schnee's favorite personal portrait: taken when he arrived for the first time in Brest, July 19, 1941.
LB

The school sailing ship *Gorch Fock* on which the young student officers spend three months learning the rudiments of life at sea. *LB*

Intense Training

After finishing high school Adalbert Schnee, born in Berlin on December 31, 1913, enlisted in the *Reichsmarine*, in April 1934 when he was twenty-years-old. His formation began with a very difficult training course in the infantry at Stralsund, which aimed at selecting officer candidates of the future *Crew 34*, of which only one out of twenty-five would be retained – there would only be 388 out of the thousands of applicants. Adalbert Schnee was very athletic, especially in nautical sports and he passed the tests without any problems.

He gained his first experience at sea during three months aboard the *Gorch Fock* training ship, where he learnt the rudiments of life at sea. At the end of the course, on September 26, 1934, he received the grade of naval cadet (*Seekadett*) and the next day embarked on the *Emden*, a light training cruiser. With the other *Crew 34* officer-candidates, he followed a nine-month training course on board which ended in September 1935. The exercises during the course included firing with real ammunition. During this period, on July 1, 1935, he was promoted to the grade of *Fähnrich zur See*. During the entire cruise the Emden's commander was a certain *Fregattenkapitän* Karl Dönitz, former ace of the U-boat corps during the First World War, who was destined to become head of the "1st U-boat Flotilla Weddigen" as soon as he reached land on September 22, 1935!

Baltic Sea, summer 1934, the young Adalbert Schnee, aged twenty, enlisted as an officer candidate in the German Navy since April, is wearing a beret bearing the inscription, "Naval School Ship *Gorch Fock*." *LB*

When he disembarked, Adalbert Schnee spent nine months on his first midshipman's theoretical course, at the Naval Academy Mürwik, the prestigious naval officers' school (located at Mürwik which is a part of Germany's most northern city, Flensburg), known as "The Chateau." During this time, his course was interrupted twice, each time for a week, so that he could follow navigation training aboard surface ships – the minesweeper *Frauenlob* and the ancillary ship *Hecht*. After the general formation that finished at the end of March 1936, he stayed on for a month and a half at Mürwik to follow a course specializing in torpedoes.

After that, he spent fifteen days at Wilhelmshaven learning about anti-aircraft defense and then on to Kiel for a week to learn about barrage weapons. During the summer of 1936, he returned to Mürwik for three weeks' training in transmission to get his radio-officer diploma, following which he spent the same amount of time in Stralsund on a midshipman infantry course. Finally, he spent two and a half months in Kiel for a theoretical artillery course.

Young Adalbert plays the accordion to motivate his comrades during maneuvers. *LB*

September 26 1934, Schnee receives the grade of cadet, reflected by the insignia on his sleeve. *LB*

His mother, Ise Wolf, accompanies her son on his first trip on the light school cruiser *Emden*, on which he will have a nine-month training course, finishing in September 1935. *LB*

The commander of the *Emden* for this cruise was *Fregattenkapitän* Karl Dönitz, former ace of the U-boat corps during World War I. During discussions with the cadets aboard, he convinced a large number of them to join the newly born German U-boat corps, in which he had great faith. *LB*

On October 11, 1936, he embarked for a five-month training course on the light cruiser *Leipzig*, which took him to the coast of Spain, a country divided by civil war. It was while he was aboard this ship that he celebrated becoming an *Oberfähnrich zur See*, on January 1, 1937. Four months later, on April 1, 1938, he was promoted to *Oberleutnant zur See* and embarked on the same ship in the role of *Divisionsleutnant* for a two-month cruise.

Choosing the U-boat Service

After three years of training, the young *Oberleutnant zur See* Adalbert Schnee chose the U-boat corps. Doubtlessly, the discussions between the officer candidates and Commander Dönitz, during the nine-month voyage on the light cruiser *Emden*, had incited many midshipmen to join the newly born German U-boat corps. Also, during his training in *Crew 34* Schnee met a lot of future U-boat corps officers who went on to be successful in their wartime career: Erich Topp (U-57 and U-552) decorated with the Knight's Cross with Oak Leaves and Swords, the four U-boat commanders decorated, like himself, with the Knight's Cross with Oak Leaves: Carl Emmermann (U-172), Adalbert Endrass (U-46 and U-567), Friedrich Guggenberger (U-81, U-847 and U-513) and Johann Mohr (U-124), and nineteen others decorated with the Knight's Cross.

On May 21, 1937, Adalbert began a new series of training and practice on this new weapon: four months of instruction at the U-boat school (*Unterseebootschule*) at Neustadt-in-Holstein on the Baltic Sea, where he was able to maneuver using a command simulator installed in the replica of a U-boat conning tower, followed by a nine-month course at U-Flotilla Weddigen aboard U-23, a IIB-type coastal U-boat, whose commander, named at the same time as Schnee, was a certain Otto Kretschmer.

In June 1938, he returned to Mürwik for a three-week course at torpedo school (formation for Underwater Torpedo Officers *Unterwasser Torpedo Offizier*) followed by two and a half months at sea aboard U-23. A complete torpedo formation (*T-lehrgang*) found him back at Mürwik for three months until mid-December 1938.

Schnee received his first officer rank, *Fähnrich-zur-See*, on July 1, 1935. *LB*

Following his disembarkation, Schnee started on a nine-month theoretical training course at the prestigious Mürwik Naval Academy. *LB*

Midshipmen marching at Mürwik: the academy was named "The Chateau." The general courses were followed by either specialized torpedo or transpatrol training. *LB*

October 11, 1936: Midshipman Schnee embarks aboard the light cruiser *Leipzig* for a five-month training course, which will take him to the Spanish coast. *LB*

After three years of basic training, *Leutnant zur See* Adalbert Schnee joins the German U-boat corps. After four months' instruction at the submariner's academy, he embarks on September 30, 1937 on U-23 in the role of watch officer under Commander Otto Kretschmer. At that time, the first German U-boat combat Flotilla, created twenty-two years earlier at Kiel by Dönitz and baptized "*U-Flottille Weddigen*," had a total of eleven coastal IIB-type U-boats": U-9, U-11, U-13, U-14, U-17, U-19, U-20, U-21, U-22, U-23 and U-24. *LB*

U-23 returned to port on December 15, 1939 and Ensign Schnee was granted fifteen days leave. He took advantage of this to marry his fiancée Ella Lüer on December 20. *LB*

First Months at War

Schnee re-embarked on U-23 to improve his skills and was promoted to sub-lieutenant on April 1, 1939. On August 25, U-23 left on patrol, and it came back on September 4, the day after Britain and France had declared war on Germany. U-23 carried out four combat patrols until mid-December with the "Commander Kretschmer/ Schnee" tandem.

During their second patrol they sunk a British merchant ship on October 4, 1939, and Schnee received his first decoration – the Iron Cross 2nd Class on his return. On November 27, 1939, he pinned the U-boat War Badge to his left breast pocket, which he was awarded for three combat patrols carried out in wartime. A second ship was sunk on December 8, 1939: a Danish merchant ship. When he returned to the U-boat port on December 14, Adalbert Schnee was granted fifteen days leave. He took advantage of this to marry his fiancée Ella Lüer on December 20 and take her to the Krümhubel ski resort for their honeymoon. To date, it had been nearly six years since he had enlisted in the German Navy, alternating between theoretical and practical training courses.

The newlyweds' honeymoon took place at Krümhubel ski resort. Schnee, who had already taken part in five combat patrols as watch officer aboard U-23, had received the Iron Cross 2nd Class whose ribbon he wore in his buttonhole, and U-Boat War Badge, awarded after three combat patrols. *LB*

Leutnant zur See Schnee was the watch officer on U-23 commanded by Otto Kretschmer from September 30, 1937 to January 2, 1940. He took part in the U-boat's first five combat patrols in September 1939, after Britain and France declared war on Germany. In the spring of 1940, Kretschmer took over the command of U-99, with which he became the greatest submariner of World War II, with a total of forty-seven ships sunk, representing 246,794 tons, and five ships damaged. *LB*

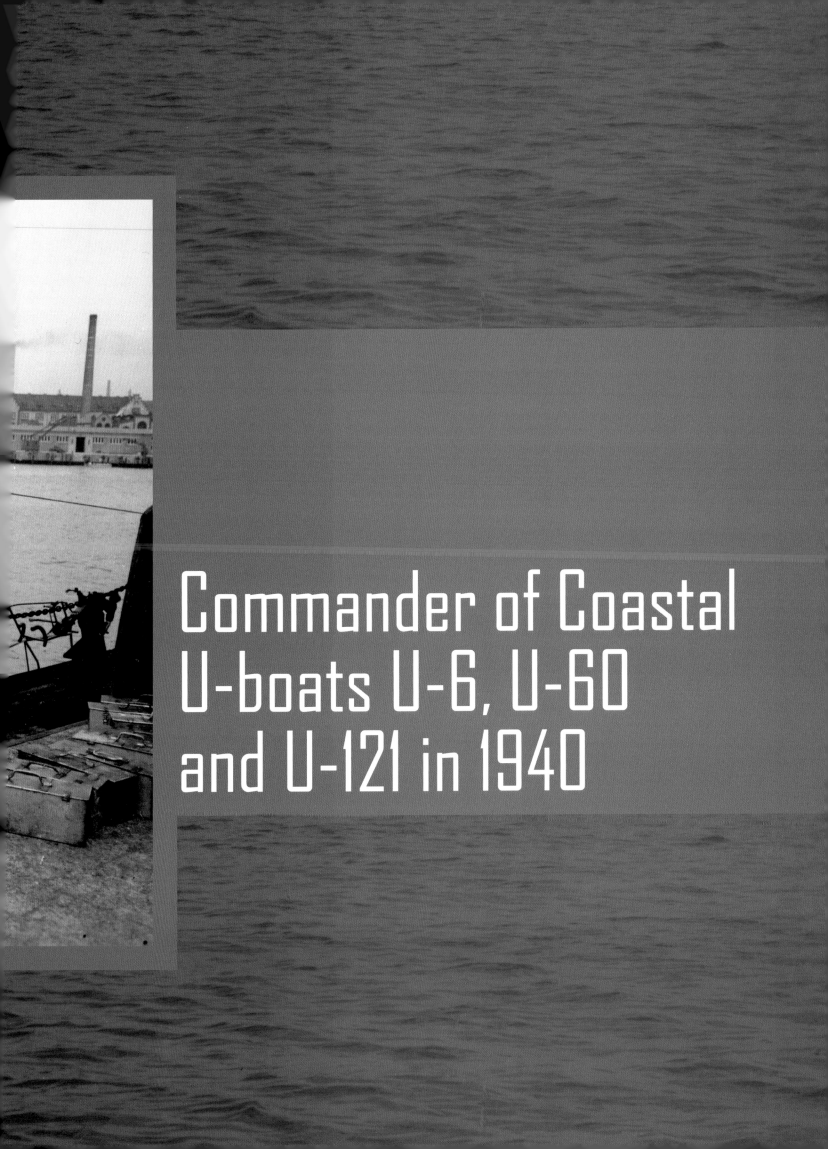

Commander of Coastal U-boats U-6, U-60 and U-121 in 1940

U-6

The New Year 1940 began, for our U-boat officer, with an appointment as commander of a U-boat, after a month of theoretical courses intended for future commanders, at the school for submariners at Neustadt. On January 30, 1940, he was officially named commander of his first U-boat, the IIA-type U-6. From April 4 to April 19, 1940, he carried out his first war patrol, taking part in the German attack on Norway: Operation *Weserübung*. Like the majority of the other U-Boats he wasn't successful, especially as his coastal U-boat was old, it had been brought into service in 1935. From mid-June to mid-July 1940, he returned to the academy for the last time for a shooting training course intended for the commanders (*Kommandantenschiessausbildung*) of the 24th Training Flotilla in Danzig.

U-60

On July 19, he took command of a IIC-type U-boat, launched in 1939, U-60 that belonged to the 1st U-boat Flotilla. This was the former "*U-Flottille Weddigen*" that U-23 belonged to and which, like the other flotillas, had been re-baptized on January 1, 1940 when it had received a number instead of a name. The U-boat had been commanded by Georg Schewe, who only managed to sink a single cargo ship after six combat patrols, and the ship wasn't hit by a torpedo but by one of the mines the U-boat had dropped four days earlier. Adalbert Schnee equalized this score on his first patrol during the first fortnight of August in the North Atlantic by torpedoing the 1,787-ton Swedish cargo ship *The Nile Gorthon*, which won him the Iron Cross 1st Class awarded on August 15. He was decorated on his arrival in Lorient on August 18. U-60's chief

On January 30, 1940, Schnee received his first appointment as commander of U-6, aboard which he carried out his first war patrol, during the attack on Norway. U-6 was an IIA-type U-boat, like U-4 in the photo where we can also see the IIB-type U-2, U-1, U-8 and U-9 belonging to the 1st Flotilla. *LB*

At the beginning of 1940, Ensign Schnee was chosen to take a U-boat commander training course at the Neustadt-in-Holstein naval school. It was there that he discovered the new tactics of attacking in a pack (wolf pack) invented by Dönitz between the wars. *LB*

engineer was *Leutnant (Ing.)* Willi Lechtenbörger. This extremely capable engineer officer stayed with his new commander for the following two years of combat.

The Command of the U-boat Corps judged this patrol from Kiel to Lorient a success in a zone particularly supervised by British aviation. The crew didn't know it, but it could have been the U-boat's last patrol: at 16:02 on August 1, off the coast of Bergen, U-60 had a near miss with two torpedoes fired in its direction by the Dutch submarine O-21; later in the day, the O-22 which also patrolled in the sector located U-boats on the surface but it was too far away to fire.

Finally, in the evening of the following day, U-60 was attacked by mistake, without damage, by a German Junkers Ju 88 aircraft that had taken off in Stavanger. Adalbert Schnee left again on operations on August 21 aboard U-60. When he returned to Lorient fifteen days later, he declared three boats sunk for a total of 24,835 tons! Actually, only the 1,401-ton British cargo ship *Ulva* was sunk; the large 15,434-ton Dutch cargo ship *Volendam* was only damaged and the third boat declared was not hit by the torpedo that was intended for it. His dogged pursuit during two days on September 2 and 3, which led to the destruction of the cargo ship *Ulva*, was appreciated as being particularly deserving for a coastal U-boat.

July 19, 1940: Schnee was appointed commander of a more modern U-boat, the IIC-type U-60. On July 30, he left the port at Kiel for a patrol in the Atlantic, to the west of Scotland. Having sunk his first ship as a commander, he arrived in Lorient on August 18, 1940, where he received the Iron Cross 1st Class. *LB*

After his second patrol aboard U-60, Commander Schnee arrives to give his report to the U-boat corps command, situated in Paris, on September 7, 1940. *Vizeadmiral* Dönitz, accompanied by his adjutant, follows the patrol's course on a sea chart. *LB*

Commander Schnee explains the details of his fifteen-day patrol. In front of him, attached to the General Staff of command of the U-boat corps, is *Kapitänleutnant* Karl Daublebsky von Eichain, former commander of U-13 and behind him is *Kapitänleutnant* Werner Winter, future chief of the 1st Flotilla in Brest in July 1942. *LB*

At the dock in Kiel, U-60's conning tower displays four pennants representing four ships this U-boat has declared to have sunk. In truth, only three of them were sunk for a total of 7 561 tons. The Dutch 15,434-ton cargo ship had been torpedoed but was only damaged and was able to reach a British port and undergo repairs. *LB*

His third and final combat patrol on U-60 took him from Lorient on September 16, 1940 to Kiel on October 8, via Bergen in Norway, this time without success. On his arrival in Germany, U-60's conning tower had the number 41,000 painted on it, the estimated total sum of tonnage sunk during U-60's nine combat patrols, which was a very exaggerated figure; actually, it was 7,561 tons with one damaged 15,434-ton ship, which for a IIC-type coastal U-boat was already an exploit in itself.

U-121

From November 6 to November 27, to keep his hand in, he commanded the IIB-type U-121 U-boat school. Moreover, at the end of the year 1940, the 1st U-Flotilla lost all its IIC and IID-type U-boats that were transformed into training boats. Still based in Kiel at the beginning of 1941, the flotilla waited for the arrival of the new VIIC-type U-boats that were progressively delivered as soon as they were finished. The first was U-201 – for Adalbert Schnee!

After returning to Kiel on October 8, 1940, following his third combat patrol, Commander Schnee poses in front of U-60's conning tower, on which the tonnage of 41,000 tons of Allied merchant ships declared sunk has been painted, along with a proverb: *"Ein Strammes Tierchen ist die Katze"* ("the cat is a strong little animal"). *LB*

If the 41,000 tons sunk is an exaggeration, that of 42,000 is correct – it refers to the number of fried eggs eaten by the crews during their patrols! *LB*

Commissioning and Patrols in U-201

Part of the crew having a break on the "winter garden" during U-201 trials in the Baltic Sea in the first quarter of 1941. The men are wearing grey leather uniforms; some of them have a miniature of the U-boat emblem attached to their garrison caps, which is that of their patron city, Remscheid. *LB*

Commissioning of U-201

On December 16, 1940, young *Oberleutnant zur See* Schnee, fresh from his experience as Watch Officer on U-23 and his success as commander of U-60, was chosen to follow the last phase of construction of the new U-201, fifteen days before celebrating his twenty-seventh birthday. It was during the year and half aboard this modern U-boat adapted to the harsh climate of the Atlantic that he showed his aptitude for command and obtained the highest decoration of the time.

To help him during patrols, Commander Schnee chose his former chief engineer on U-60, *Leutnant (Ing.)* Willi Lechtenbörger; his watch officer was *Oberleutnant zur See* Karl-Horst Horn and the 3rd officer was *Leutnant zur See* Wolfgang Leimkühler. First of all, during a month and a half, the commander and his crew took part in the final assembly of their future U-boat with the workmen of the *Friedrich Krupp Germania Werft* shipyard in Kiel-Gaarden. During this assembly period, they got to know every bolt, cable and pipe of their U-boat. They even knew the parts and mechanisms that would be hidden by the future floor, which would be very useful in the event of any technical problems while on patrol.

During a solemn ceremony on January 25, 1941, in presence of the crew and workmen having taken part in the work, U-201 was officially given to *Kriegsmarine* by the shipyards and declared as being brought into service. The Mayor and the representatives of Remscheid, known as the sea town in the mountains, were also present for the ceremony. It was U-201's patron town where the crew would stay during leave periods.

Launching ceremony for U-201 on January 25, 1941. The naval shipyards *Krupp Germania Werft* of Kiel officially hand over the U-boat to the *Kriegsmarine*. From left to right: *Oberleutnant zur See* Karl-Horst Horn the watch officer, Lieutenant (engineers) Willi Lechtenbörger, chief engineer, *Oberleutnant zur See* Commander Adalbert Schnee, *Leutnant zur See* Wolfgang Leimkühler, third officer. *LB*

Commander Schnee directs operations using a megaphone. When he received his Knight's Cross, this photo was printed in Germany in large numbers as a postcard, because at that time, commanders so decorated were national heroes. *LB*

Baltic Sea Exercise

U-201 was launched, but that didn't mean that it would immediately leave on combat patrols; it had to be tried out and the U-boat and crew were sent to the Baltic Sea where they stayed for two and a half months. The first tests were carried out between January 26-30, 1941 by the U-boat Acceptance Commission (*UAK* [*Unterseeboot Abnahme Kommando*]). Based in Kiel, this department was charged with testing U-201's resistance and waterproofing when it dived as well as making sure the radio equipment worked properly.

During the first twelve days of February the crew underwent intensive training aboard, then the *UAK* did another series of tests until February 27 with a second test-dive on February 13; a return to the shipyards from February 14 to February 17 for repairs, following technical problems detected during the dive. On February 18, exercise torpedoes were loaded and fired on the following day, followed by the third test-dive. The *UAK* tests finished on February 27, 1941. On March 4, after a few days of additional tests in Kiel while waiting for the Baltic Sea to thaw out, U-201, along with three other U-boats, left for Danzig. It spent a week with the 25th Training Flotilla, subjected to the U-boat

Acceptance Group (*UAG* (*Unterseeboot Abnahme Gruppe*)) tests: at sea it carried out a series of exercises and artillery firing on the surface with its 88mm gun. From March 11 to March 15, U-201 was attached to Gotenhafen Port, site of the 27th Front –line Training Flotilla, where it passed torpedo tests at sea with the Torpedo Testing Commission (*TEAK* (*Torpedoerprobungskommando*)).

Once all these tests had been passed with success, it spent fifteen days in training with the technical training group for front-line U-boats (*Agru-Front* (*Ausbildungsgruppe für U-Boote Front*)): with other U-boats also in training they carried out simulated wolf-pack attacks on a false enemy convoy: cargo ships escorted by battleships with the participation of aviation.

After that, U-201 returned to Danzig Bay from March 16 to 25, where real torpedoes were fired off night and day; then off the coast of Gotenhafen from March 25 to April 3 for the last tactical exercises of wolfpack attacking.

After this period of tests and intensive exercises, U-201 went back to the *Germania Werft* shipyard in Kiel for a week of revision, following which it was really ready to be sent out on combat patrols.

On April 22, 1941, U-201 left the port at Kiel for its first combat patrol, in the direction of Iceland. *LB*

Compass Failure

On April 19, 1941, in Kiel, U-201's hull was demagnetized, fourteen torpedoes were loaded on board along with food. A last test-dive was carried out the day before departure. U-201 left Kiel Port on April 22, in direction of the south of Iceland.

On April 26, at the beginning of the afternoon, the gyroscopic compass stopped functioning; the commander gave the order to dive, to try to repair it in peace, but without success. The U-boat resurfaced at 20:15, the problem couldn't be resolved on board. The radio operator was ordered to send a message to the U-boat Corps Command: the U-boat had to stop in Bergen in Norway, where it arrived the following day at 10:40. While waiting for the specialist in gyroscopic compasses, who was on a business trip in Oslo, U-201 refilled the tanks with fuel and took on board more food and water. The compass was finally, more-or-less, repaired, and the U-boat left Bergen on April 29 at 23:00.

First Combat

The following day, a first air raid warning sounded at midday, and it dived immediately! Resurfacing at 12:15, U-201 continued on its course. A new air raid warning sounded at 14:04, a new dive of fifteen minutes before resurfacing and continuing on its way.

On April 30, it was slowed up once again by a third air raid warning at 20:50! The passage to the north of the British Isles was not without risk. At midnight, the Shetland Islands were in sight – then the Faroe Islands at midday on May 1. At 17:28, the radio operator intercepted a coded message from

U-boat Corps Command HQ (*BdU*): "At 10:00, a convoy was announced in the AN 1321 square to the west." The commander worked out their position; it was attainable! The U-boat left at full speed on the surface, heading west. At 09:51 on May 2, a new radio message came from the *BdU* and the commander gave the order to get into attacking position in the AL11- AL22 square. Suddenly, at 18:40, an oil tanker on its own was sighted! It had been damaged and its engines were stopped. U-201 dived because a 120mm gun was spotted on the back of the tanker; the U-boat approached its goal using its electric motors. At 21:14, it launched a seventh torpedo from a distance of 1,500 meters on the ship that was identified as being the 8,190-ton British tanker *Capulet*. The torpedo hit its objective but it still didn't sink! U-201 resurfaced and 88mm shells were fired from the onboard gun one after the other. It took fifty-four shots and the tanker from the HX 121 convoy, which had been damaged by U-552 on April 28 and abandoned, finally sank. It was U-201's first victim.

The U-boat continued on its way towards the sector that was indicated by the U-boat Corps Command, in front of the convoy that had left the British Isles heading west. A radio message from the *BdU* at 00:16 on May 3 ordered U-boat to the AL 15 square which it reached at 04:00 the following morning. At that moment it intercepted a message from U-552 indicating a strong traffic of ships in the 52 to 43 AM squares, to the east of its position. At 20:36, another radio message was received, this time from U-96, which reported a convoy in the AE 3457 square. Commander Schnee worked out positions, but the convoy was too far north to be reached.

On May 5, at 03:30, U-201, that had reached the AL 1951 square, spotted a large steamer on the port side! As the night was very clear, it approached as near as 2,000 meters and decided to fire a torpedo on the surface at a distance of forty miles. But as soon as the torpedo was fired, the ship, which was identified as being a large modern 10,000-12,000-ton steamer, veered off showing its back end to the U-boat and the torpedo missed the ship! In spite of the distance the U-boat had been spotted; the steamer sped up to 17-18 knots and slowly disappeared. The U-boat chased it until 09:00 in the morning, but couldn't catch up with it. The commander decided to return to square AL19.

A problem with the gyroscope compass forced the commander to make a stop in Bergen Port from April 27-29 for repairs. *LB*

Atlantic Convoy OB 318

On May 6 at 17:44, a radio message reported that a plane had spotted a convoy in the AL 3159 square, the U-boat travelled at once towards the north. On May 7 between 02:15 and 14:30, because of a very calm sea, the torpedo that was in reserve under the upper bridge was lowered to the front compartment. At 21:16, a radio message transmitted by U-94 reported a convoy in the AE 7772 square, to the south of Iceland (convoy OB 318, which had left Liverpool on May 2 heading west, with thirty-eight boats).

Commander Schnee deducing that it was the same convoy spotted by the day before turned U-201 in its direction. By midday on May 8, no new message arrived concerning this convoy, and Commander Schnee decided to advance slowly towards the east. Suddenly at 13:30, the convoy was sighted!

At 13:36, the U-boat dived to attack. In the periscope the commander saw a convoy of four columns of twenty-five to thirty cargo ships, escorted from afar by five to six destroyers and several other battleships as additional protection. A *Sunderland* seaplane circled above the convoy. The ships on the starboard side were particularly well protected, because large 10,000 to 16,000 ton battleships were on that side. U-201 slipped amongst the convoy ships and fired at a 6,000 to 8,000-ton ship; the torpedo reached its target making a large "clang"! It didn't seem to have exploded, was it defective?

Three other torpedoes were then fired at targets from 300 to 1,200 meters away, but the commander had problems seeing the targets clearly through the periscope! Oil prevented him from being able to pinpoint them precisely; the ships seemed to have been cut into several pieces! The periscope was lowered and the oil pumped off, but when it was raised the waterline was no longer in sight – firing was impossible.

As the commander knew that the destroyers escorted the convoy from twenty to thirty miles in front and behind, he decided to dive to a depth of fifty meters and to resurface once the convoy gained fifty miles. At 20:20 it resurfaced and saw the convoy in the distance. A radio message was sent giving his new position and then he took up the hunt. On May 9, at 10:30, the convoy was spotted again on the port side. U-201 wasn't alone in the attack.

U-110's Engima Falls into British Hands

At U-201's side was U-*boat West Pack* one of which was Commander Lemp's U-110, with whom messages are exchanged on the surface by signals from conning tower to conning tower between 12:15 and 12:30. It was agreed that U-110 would strike first while U-201 waited to take over the attack. U-110 disappeared; it came into contact with the convoy and attacked! After having succeeded in sinking two ships, it was forced to resurface after being attacked by depth charges. The commander Lemp ordered the crew to abandon the U-boat where destructive charges had been placed.

A British team from the destroyer *HMS Bulldog* took possession of the U-boat, which didn't explode because the charges didn't function. The British recovered invaluable booty on board: an *Enigma* machine with its rollers, codebooks, and charts.

This incredible catch was transmitted to the decoding service at Bletchley Park, which in a few weeks enabled them to decode the radio messages from the German battleships then the three rotor Enigma machines belonging to U-boats by the end of the year. U-110, whose commander had been killed, was towed by the destroyer *Bulldog* but finally on May 10 it sank.

Firing the 20mm anti-aircraft gun. During its first patrol U-201 was forced to dive three times on April 30, 1941, following the appearance of a plane while sailing through the highly risky passage above the British Isles. *LB*

In the U-boat, the mess cook only had a small working area next to one of the two lavatories, to prepare meals for the crew. *LB*

The stove had three electric warming plates, the utensils were made of aluminum and the crockery was porcelain. *LB*

U-201 Continues Patrol

During this time, U-201 was unaware of U-110's fate. At 12:54, faced with the distant arrival of two destroyers, Commander Schnee decided not to dive to fire his torpedoes. He decided to attack on the surface and advanced towards the convoy. At 14:26, he launched two torpedoes at an interval of ten seconds towards a 12,000-ton transporter located at a distance of 1,700 meters. Two detonations were heard after 117 seconds, with a ten second interval. At 14:28, he fired a torpedo from the back tube, towards a 6,000-ton steamer, and then immediately dived to twenty-five meters.

Payback quickly arrived! From 14:30 to 19:05, U-201 was chased by the two destroyers that dropped ninety-nine depth charges!

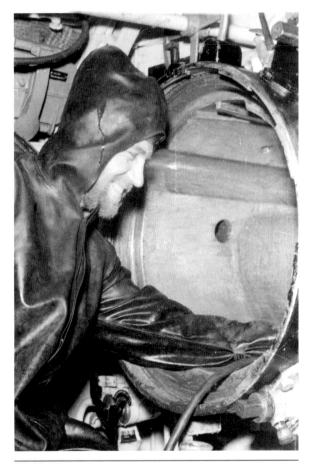

During a patrol, a large part of the time was spent doing cleaning and maintenance; especially the five torpedo firing tubes (four in front, one in back). *LB*

A little after midday on May 9, not far from a convoy, U-201 exchanged signals with Commander Lemp of U-110. A few hours later this U-boat was boarded by a British crew from *HMS Bulldog*, who captured its Enigma machine and precious coding documents. *IWM*

Obermechanikermaat Adolf Dölle supervises placing an "eel" (as the crew nicknamed torpedoes) into its firing tube. *LB*

Finally the attacks stopped and calm was restored; at 23:15 the U-boat resurfaced to take stock of the damage. It was heavy on many apparatuses, the pressure gauges, compass and torpedo releasing systems; some batteries were broken, two antenna cables were cut, and the sonar was out of order.

On May 10, at 03:12, the commander of U-201 sent a radio message to the *BdU* to report that he had sunk a 12,000-ton transport and a 6,000-ton cargo ship. He estimated to be able to repair the U-boat's essential damage by May 12.

Dangerous Oil Leak

Finally he sent a second message at 19:11 to report an oil leak from a torn external fuel tank. The reply from the *BdU* arrived at 20:41: "*in the event of visible oil leakage, make a half-turn towards Lorient.*" On May 11 at 04:00, the commander thought that the oil leak came only from one tank. He decided to carry on his patrol by initially using the fuel from this tank and in the case of an emergency he would have it quickly emptied overboard.

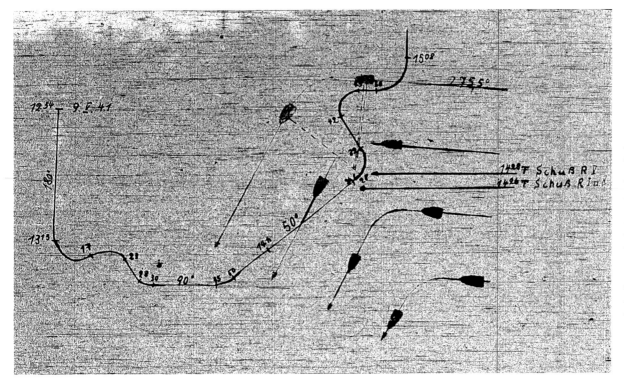

A sketch in U-201's logbook specifies the torpedo firing sequence against merchant ships in convoy OB 318 on May 9, 1941. The first two, tubes I and II at 14:26, then a third two minutes later from the tube in back when the U-boat turned round. Two ships were hit; one was sunk while the other was only damaged.

At 11:50, boat-vapor was sighted in the distance! U-201 dived but the vapor slowly decreased.

The U-boat resurfaced, the commander decided to go on ahead of his target. At 16:00 more vapor was sighted, U-201 reported the position of this convoy by radio: AK 1864 square, heading southwest. But at 20:03, when the *BdU* gave the authorization to attack and U-201 was in a good position to fire from a dive, a very dense fog rolled across the sea. Visibility fell by fifty meters to only 100 meters.

Twice the *BdU* sent a message to the U-boat asking whether it was headed towards Lorient following its oil leakage, each time the answer was: "no."

On May 12 at 12:00, visibility was clear again and the U-boat headed out to search for the convoy of the day before. But it continued to lose oil, which was very dangerous because it made them easy to locate.

Commander Schnee decided to empty the external tanks one after the other into the sea to try to stop the oil leakage. The following day at 08:00, the leak was still there, it must have come from an interior tank. The commander decided to head back to Lorient. On May 14 at 05:40, it met up with U-74. The two U-boats tried to sink a steamer, but in vain. (The U-74 continued its patrol during that it was sent in search of survivors from the battleship *Bismarck* sunk on May 27; it found only three.).

After firing U-201 dives. Payback comes in the form of two destroyers that drop ninety-nine depth charges in the direction of the U-boat which suffers a little damage. Chief Engineer Willi Lechtenbörger, wearing his life jacket, counts the hits. *UBA*

Adalbert Schnee, the commander of U-201, returns to the port at Lorient, where he has been twice before when he was the commander of U-60. *LB*

U-201 arrived in Lorient at midday on May 18. The report/ratio, stated to have sunk four boats totaling 26,000 tons. Actually, it sank three boats for 16,010 tons (the 8,190-ton British tanker *Capulet* on May 2, 1941, the 2,018-ton French cargo ship Kervegan on May 8 that it thought it had missed because of a defective torpedo and the 5,802 ton British cargo ship *Gregalia* May 9), and damaged a fourth (the 5,969-ton British cargo ship *Worsen Cloud* on May 9).

The *BdU* noted in its assessment that it was a well-led patrol, mainly in the attack on the convoy. The U-boat stayed for three weeks in the Lorient shipyards for repair and maintenance. This was the first operational port to receive U-boats on the French coast since July 1940. When Brest began to be operational in July 1941, it accommodated the units of the 1st Flotilla.

On May 18, 1941, U-201 arrives at Lorient, to be welcomed by the army's brass band that is set up on the former escort ship *Isère,* used as a pontoon across the Scorff River in front of the Péristyle Barracks. *UBA*

Empty-handed Because of Fog

June 8, 1941, in the Lorient Scorff, U-201 passes U-123, commanded by Reinhard Hardegen, which is also leaving on operations. This U-boat in an IXB-type, larger and on which the exterior ballasts aren't prominent. *UBA*

The U-201's second patrol, leaving Lorient on June 8, 1941, took it to the west of Ireland following a radio message from the *BdU* received six days after its departure, indicating that an Italian submarine had located a convoy in the BE 18 square. In spite of an active searching by several U-boats of the *Kurfürst* Wolf Pack, in the square 39, to the west of the reported convoy, no allied ship was seen. U-201 left the pack on June 21. Two days later, a radio message transmitted by U-203 reported a convoy to the south of Greenland, sailing slowly towards the east. This was the HX 133 convoy of fifty-one cargo ships, which had left Halifax on June 16 for Liverpool. Commander Schnee decided to head for this sector. On the way on the same day, at 17:50 it saw a fast steamer that increased its speed to seventeen knots. It chased it on the surface, but the fog suddenly became increasingly dense. Visibility oscillated between 3,000 and 5,000 meters. When U-201 was 3,000 meters from the steamer, visibility fell to only

1,500 meters. At 23:45, U-201 dived to fire from below the surface, but visibility fell to 1,000 meters, and Commander Schnee couldn't see anything through the periscope. He decided to resurface at 23:59 but didn't manage to find the steamer that had been too rapid.

Vain Pursuit of Convoy HX 133

He headed for the HX 133 convoy, again reported by a radio message from U-556 on June 26 at 12:49, this time in the AK 1425 square. On the way, U-201 was forced to crash- dive June 26 at 22:03 then on June 27 at 00:33 following the appearance of a Sunderland seaplane. At 02:00 in the morning, an explosion was heard in the distance, it moved in closer to the reported convoy. At 02:35, the convoy was in front of him, but was supervised by two planes. The fog was dense and at 03:30 visibility didn't exceed 2,000 meters. Accompanied by U-556, U-201 approached the convoy on the surface.

At 04:00, U-556 dived and left. The same day, chased for more than seven hours and bombarded by depth charges from three British corvettes, this U-boat was forced to resurface, and immediately came under the fire from Allied guns what that caused, in addition to the loss of the U-boat, five dead among the crew.

Whereas, U-201, still on the surface, tried not to lose the convoy, when suddenly, at 07:38, an alarm sounded! A seaplane appeared from the clouds and dropped five bombs in direction of the U-boat,

The crew of U-201 salutes the crew of U-123. On the camouflaged conning tower, we can see the emblem that represents the coat of arms of their patron city of Remscheid. Bouquets of flowers cover each of the conning towers as well as the top of the periscope. A pie and lobsters have been put on the front of U-123's conning tower! *UBA*

Searching for balance while diving with one of the ballast command valves. *LB*

One of the numerous ballast command shutters, the whole of which is nicknamed "Christmas tree" by the crew. *LB*

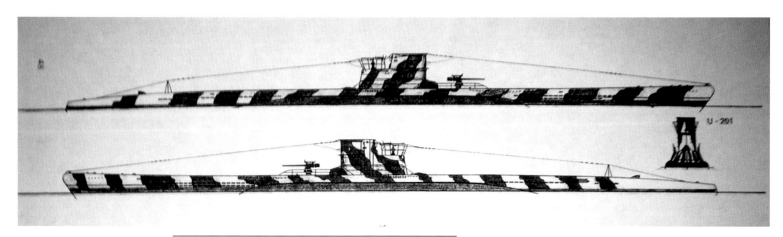

The camouflage of U-201 is painted zebra stripes. *DR*

The crew is lined up on the front bridge; their commander is going to meet his flotilla chief. *LB*

On U-201's bridge, Commander Schnee is talking with the chief of the 1st U-boat Flotilla, *Korvettenkapitän* Hans Cohausz. This officer came to Brest for the first time in March 1941 to have a look around the new fortifications. On June 7, he sent a train with fifteen wagons from Kiel to Brest, to transport the NCOs and privates from his flotilla with spare parts for the U-boats. On June 13, a Junkers Ju 52 plane took him to the Guipavas Airport along with his officers and engineers of his General Staff. The train with the rest of the material arrived two days later. Then all the personnel of the flotilla settled into the Saint-Pierre-Quilbignon naval academy. The officers were housed in the central building that was 298 meters long, the troops in the outbuildings, mainly in the equipment barracks. The 1st U-boat Flotilla's administration staff requisitioned other buildings, notably the Astoria Hotel in the town center, which had been transformed into a community club home for the submariners (*U-Bootskameradschaftsheim*). *UBA*

July 19, 1941, U-201 arrives in Penfeld River after an unsuccessful patrol in the North Atlantic. U-201's logbook has the details of the approach: July 19 at 07:20, Point *"Stern – star"* reached; 11:00, taken in charge by two patrol boats at point 32; 13:00 reception by the blockade runner 19:15 arrival at Brest. *ECPAD*

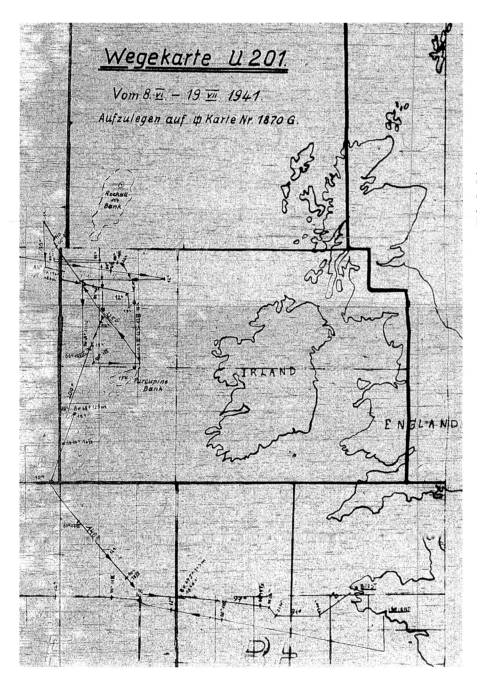

Chart taken from U-201's logbook, showing the area off the coast of Ireland covered by the patrol between June 8 and July 19, 1941, from the departure from Lorient to the arrival at Brest. *UBA*

which suffered very slight damage. At 08:30 it resurfaced, but U-201 was forced to dive again because of the same plane five minutes later. It resurfaced at 08:55 and set out again with after the convoy, which was still supervised by at least one plane. At 15:00, the commander decided to go on ahead of the convoy at full speed, while remaining at a distance of thirty miles. But at 01:00 on June 28, the commander had a radio message sent to the *BdU* announcing that since 15:00 the previous day an attack was impossible because of a very dense fog.

U-201 had to abandon the pursuit. The HX 133 convoy had five ships sunk by U-203, U-564 and U-651 between June 24 and June 29 and two damaged. But, because of the fog and air cover, U-201 was not able to get into a good firing position.

Nurse Gretel, of German Red Cross, distributes a small gift for everyone. From the bottom: 2nd officer *Oberleutnant zur See* Karl Horst Horn, the engineer Willi Lechtenbörger, 3rd Officer and helmsman Wolfgang Leimkühler, and *OberSteuermann* Karl Boddenberg. Uniform are very simple and devoid of the national emblem. All wear caps with the Remscheid coat-of-arms, their U-boat's patron city. *UBA*

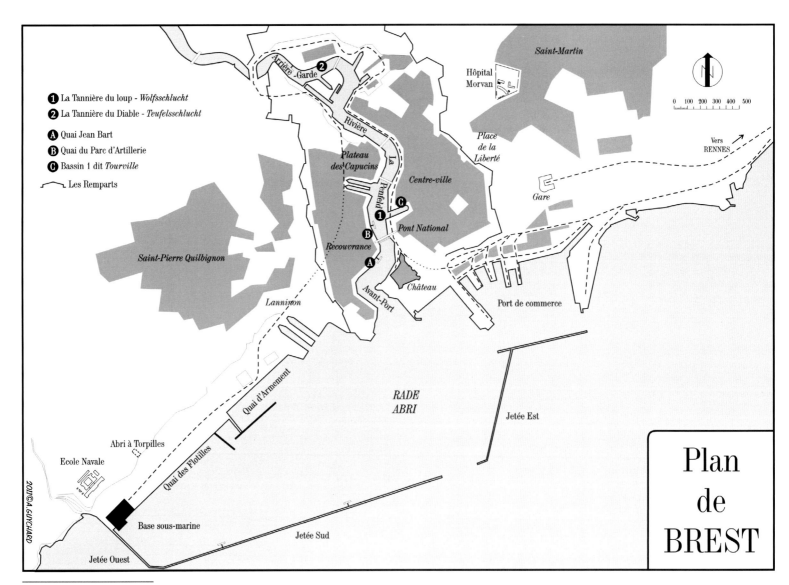

Plan of the German installations at Brest.
Drawing by Anthony Guychard

Legend:
1. La Tannière du loup - *Wolfsschlucht*
2. La Tannière du Diable - *Teufelsschlucht*
A. Quai Jean Bart
B. Quai du Parc d'Artillerie
C. Bassin 1 dit *Tourville*
— Les Remparts

U-201 has just berthed alongside quay "Jean Bart," just in front of the access door of the same name. On the pontoon above, the officers of the 1st Flotilla along with about a dozen female auxiliaries from the army service are ready to greet the crew. On the lower level in the centre, a nurse in white is waiting to offer the traditional bouquet of flowers to the commander. The rest of the troops have remained on the quay. Behind the camouflaged ships on the right, is the Tanguy tower. *ECPAD*

Inside the naval academy, the large canteen used to welcome the crews returning from patrols, is decorated with a fresco to remind the submariners of the 1st Flotilla's first home port: it represents the German navy memorial in Kiel-Laboe, built at the end of the First World War, in front of which a U-boat is passing, and surmounted by a war proverb: "Comrades! Never forget: attack – as close as possible – sink!" *LB*

Towards Brest

After a new air raid warning on July 7 then the unfruitful search for a convoy sighted by the *Luftwaffe* the same day, U-201's lookouts set off the alarm five times for planes until July 12. On July 14 at 20:00, Commander Schnee announced to the crew that their U-boat would be heading back to France. On July 15, and again on July 16, they once again spotted a plane, then on July 17 they received a radio message from the *BdU* ordering them back to Brest.

On July 19, U-201 arrived for the first time in the 1st Flotilla's new homeport with all its torpedoes, without success, in spite of a patrol of 6,485 miles. Of this patrol the U-boat Corps Command

AUTHOR'S NOTE: U-201's logbooks, although existing for all the following patrols, are unfortunately of very bad quality. Reading them properly has proved impossible. The 3rd, 4th, 5th, 6th and 7th patrols carried out by this U-boat under the command of Adalbert Schnee will thus be described less precisely.

German map showing Brest Port and the surrounding area. The U-boat base that is to be established to the west of the military port should be able to harbour twelve U-boats by the end of 1941. *LB*

commented that the commander had done everything he could, and that the bad luck to have seen almost no enemy ships would not last.

U-201 stayed for a month in the shipyards in Brest for maintenance. The watch officer who had seconded Commander Schnee for U-201's first two combat patrols, *Oberleutnant zur See* Karl-Horst Horn, left the U-boat to follow training courses intended for future commanders. As the commander of U-705 he died at sea to the west of Brest on September 3 1942. He was replaced on board U-201 by *Oberleutnant zur See* Joachim Zander. The 3rd officer remained *Leutnant zur See* Wolfgang Leimkühler.

At the end of the second patrol, Karl-Horst Horn, the watch officer aboard U-201 since the beginning of the year, left the U-boat. He was sent to Germany to follow a commanders' training course. He was the commander of U-705 when he was killed west of Brest on September 3, 1942. He was replaced aboard U-201 by *Oberleutnant-zur-See* Joachim Zander. *LB*

U-201 left Brest on August 14, 1941 for its third combat patrol, in the direction of the Atlantic to intercept convoys sailing from Liverpool to Gibraltar. *LB*

Objective: Convoy OG 71

U-201 left Brest on August 14, 1941 heading for the North Atlantic. On August 17, the OG 71 convoy was reported to the west of Ireland. This convoy, which left Liverpool on August 13 for Gibraltar, comprised twenty-one merchant ships. U-201 succeeded finding it in the evening of August 17 and tracked it until the first hours of August 19; at 04:06, it launched a salvo of four torpedoes in its direction. Two detonations against a presumed 12,000-ton oil tanker, and two others against cargo ships were heard. Actually, it "almost" sank the 1,809-ton British cargo ship *Ciscar* that was finished off by U-204 an hour later. On the other hand it sank the 3,255-ton *Aguila*.

They lost sight of the convoy the following day. Although spotted by a Condor plane on August 21, U-boats didn't find it again. On August 23, U-564 spotted it and radioed U-201 for backup. On August 23 at 02:14 to the northwest of Lisbon, Commander Schnee fired four torpedoes in direction of the OG 71 convoy's remaining ships. He saw one hit a steamer and two others a tanker, which burst into flame and sank fifteen minutes later. At 02:16, a single torpedo was launched towards another commercial ship and a detonation was heard. In fact, once again, only two British cargo ships were sunk, the 787-ton *Stork* and the 1,974-ton *Aldergrove*.

At the time of this last attack, U-201's logbook recorded two other unreal successes against a 4,000-ton cargo ship and another of 8,000 tons. When U-201 arrived in Brest on August 25, 1941, it declared a total tonnage sunk during the twelve days patrol as 31,825 tons for seven ships. The reality was somewhat different; in fact only three cargo ships amounting to 6,016 tons were sunk and one of 1,809 tons was damaged.

During the night of August 18/19, U-201 managed to get into firing position on the head of the convoy it had been tracking for two days. The electric motors took over for navigation during the dive. A mechanic has put a small photo of his fiancée onto a data sheet. *LB*

On August 17, a convoy was signaled to the west of Ireland. The commander ordered the mechanic in charge of the port diesel motor to put the machines on full speed ahead. *LB*

A minesweeper opens the passage towards the Goulet de Brest. To avoid hitting a mine dropped by the British, U-201 follows in its wake. *LB*

Knight's Cross

However, these declarations were held to be true by the General Staff, and after the third patrol on U-201 Commander Schnee, who had already sunk several ships while on U-60, passed the theoretical bar of 100,000 tons of cargo ships sunk. This earned him the Knight's Cross, the first to be awarded in Brest. This decoration was personally pinned to his chest on August 30 by *Vizeadmiral* Karl Dönitz who had arrived two days earlier for his first visit to the 1st Flotilla. He also awarded the Iron Cross to several submariners who had taken part in the attack on the OG 71 convoy. The U-boat Corps Command appreciated the very successful patrol that proved that a well-commanded U-boat could be successful even against well-defended convoys.

Map of U-201's third patrol from August 14-25, taken from its logbook. *UBA*

Commander Schnee sitting on the edge of the conning tower. *UBA*

Inscriptions destined for the welcome committee have been painted on the conning tower: "Stich Ich ihn noch einmal" – "I stung him one more time" *UBA*

On August 25, 1941, a large ceremony was held for U-201's return, fresh from its attack on the OG 71 convoy. Its commander, having theoretically passed the symbolic bar of 100,000 tons of shipping sunk, was awarded the Knight's Cross by Dönitz on August 30 in Brest. *LB*

The end of August 1941: at that time the man nicknamed "Adi" Schnee was the second commander of the 1st Flotilla after "Teddy" Suhren (on the left), to be awarded the Knight's Cross. He could now start signing autographs, a widespread tradition in that era after receiving this award. *LB*

On August 30, 1941, a war correspondent interviews the two aces of the 1st Flotilla decorated with the Knight's Cross. Teddy Suhren and Adi Schnee are only, respectively, twenty-five and twenty-seven years old. Both will leave for new patrols on September 14 and 16. *LB*

Sitting on the footboard of a general staff car, the war correspondent records Schnee's story. U-201's logbook details its maintenance in Brest: August 26: Taken into the shipyard; September 1: put into a dry dock; September 9: trial course and demagnetization of the hull; September 11: loading torpedoes and ammunition; September 12: loading provisions; September 13: final trial course and loading fresh foodstuffs; September 14: departure for the fourth patrol. *LB*

U-201 left Brest on September 14, 1941, for its fourth combat patrol. A lookout searches for a convoy in the middle of the Atlantic. *LB*

Success Against Convoy OG 74 …

After three weeks of maintenance, on September 14, 1941, U-201 left Brest in direction of the west of Ireland. On the way on September 20, it intercepted a message from U-124 reporting a convoy moving towards the north of the Azores. This was the OG 74 convoy, which had left Liverpool on September 12, for Gibraltar, and comprised twenty-two merchant ships. Commander Schnee calculated that he could get to the reported sector.

Indeed the convoy was spotted that same evening, but U-201 was kept at a distance and even forced to dive following the appearance of a *Martlet* fighter plane that had taken off from the escort carrier *HMS Audacity*. It was followed by the sloop *HMS Deptford,* and the corvette *HMS Arbutus.*

But Commander Schnee wouldn't abandon the chase, and found the OG 74 convoy in the evening of September 21, 800 miles north of the Azores. Between 22:50 and 23:41, it successively fired four torpedoes that sank the three British cargo ships *Runa, Smoothed* and *Rhineland,* respectively 1,575, 1,511 and 1,381 tons. Contact was lost with the convoy the following day.

… Then Against Convoy HG 73

But U-124 and U-201 found another convoy coming the opposite way, the HG 73 which had left Gibraltar on September 17, for Liverpool, with twenty-five cargo ships. In the early hours of September 27, U-201 launched its attack: at 02:06, it fired two torpedoes one which hit a cargo ship which would have sunk and the other an auxiliary protection ship. In fact, only the 5,155-ton *CAM Ship* (*catapult aircraft merchant ship*) *HMS Springbank* was damaged to an extent that it was sunk by the corvette *HMS Jasmine.* At 02:09, a third torpedo was fired, but it was defective. Two minutes later, a new salvo of two torpedoes was launched; they both hit the 2,468-ton Norwegian cargo ship *Siremalm* that sank immediately. In the evening, U-201 recommenced its attack against the convoy and declared to have sunk two more cargo ships by 23:03. In fact, only the loss of the 3,103-ton British *Margareta* was confirmed.

This time, U-201, which was forced to dive as soon as it fired its torpedoes to escape the escort ships, couldn't effectively note the results, and brought back a tonnage sunk rather nearer to reality when it arrived in Brest on September 30, 1941. It carried out its most profitable patrol hitherto, with six boats destroyed from two convoys during its short seventeen-day patrol, for a total tonnage of 15,193 tons.

The U-boat Corps Command commented that the exceptional control of this short and successful patrol proved Commander Schnee's capacities.

Return to Brest

In Brest, U-201 was put in the shelter in the U-boat base which then counted five almost finished pens, which would later be numbered D, E and 1, 2 and 3. This new equipment would make it possible for the flotilla to accommodate more U-boats at the same time.

The flotilla's war diary announced that at the end of September the docking capacities in Brest only had six places. That would explain why, with the occasional arrival of U-boats from the 3rd Flotilla in Brest, several of the 1st Flotilla's U-boats were obliged to make their technical stopover in Lorient or Saint-Nazaire.

U-201 remained for a month in Brest for maintenance. Adalbert Schnee benefited from it to take leave with his family in Germany; he spent time with his wife and his first son Jürgen who was a few months old. In October, he also went to his U-boat's patron city, Remscheid, where he talked about his patrols with the population, signed the city's visitors' book and played a few pieces on the accordion. The aim of this ace submariner's visit was to promote the German U-boat corps, whose recruitment was mainly voluntary.

Leutnant zur See Wolfgang Leimkühler, 3rd officer since U-201 was launched, left the U-boat to follow the training course intended for commanders. He died in combat in the North Atlantic on February 15, 1943 as the commander of U-225. He was replaced by *Leutnant zur See* Martin Duppel.

The faithful chief engineer Willi Lechtenbörger, with the coat of arms of the patron city Remscheid on his garrison cap. *LB*

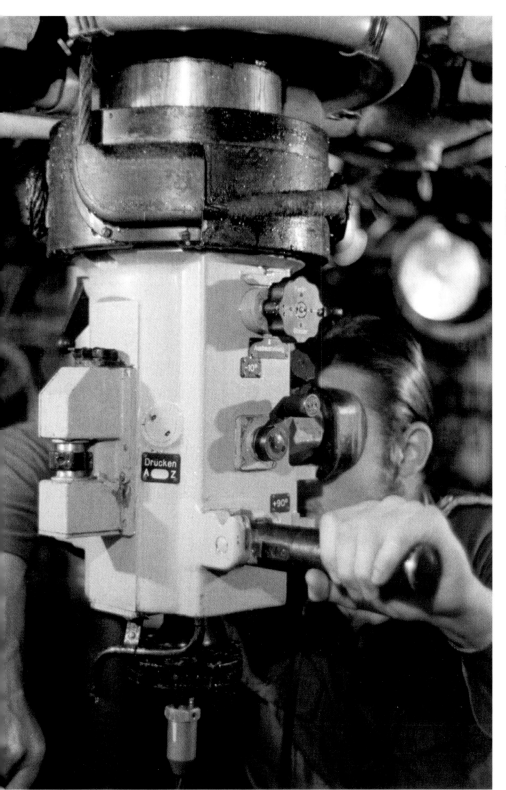

During the evening of September 21, Commander Schnee watches the convoy through the watch periscope situated in the central compartment. He will give the order to fire four torpedoes that will sink three British cargo ships. *LB*

On September 20, 1941, U-201's radio, manned by Radioman (*FunkMaat*) Hermann Klein, captures a message from U-124, reporting a convoy heading towards the north of the Azores. The commander makes some calculations – it is reachable! *LB*

The diesel engines are
pushed to the limit
to reach the reported
convoy *LR*

September 30, 1941, U-201 returns to Brest. Several officers aboard a motor launch go to meet it, notably Gunther Krech (commander of U-558) who shakes the hand of one of the crewmembers. *LB*

Bouquets of flowers in their hands, several German women await the arrival of the crew, especially Nurse Gretel who never misses this U-boat's arrival. *LB*

Commander Schnee directs the approach maneuvers through a megaphone. *LB*

Nine pennants are raised on U-201's periscope when it arrives at the Artillery Park quay in Brest on September 30, 1941. Four of them refer to the attack on the OG-74 convoy, the other five refer to the HG-73 convoy. German Nurse Gretel now on U-201's bridge along with the crew salutes the arrival of U-203. She is holding a bouquet of flowers that she will give to Commander Rolf Mützelburg. *UBA*

Preceded by a brass band from the army, U-201's crew arrives in front of the naval academy's lodge after marching through the town. *ECPAD*

On September 30, 1941, U-201's crew march through town with their victory pennants. A tram heading towards St Pierre Quilbignon is about to pass them. *ECPAD*

In October 1941, Adalbert Schnee goes to make a speech in Remscheid, the patron city of his U-boat, to persuade the adolescents of age to do their military service in the German U-boat corps. *LB*

In the theater, where young girls have given a musical recital, he thanks the town's councilmen for their welcome. *LB*

He also plays music on the accordion. *LB*

Schnee signs the town's
visitor's book. *LB*

Back at home with his son, Jürgen, aged a few
months, Adalbert changes out of his uniform, to help
him feel that he really is on leave. *LB*

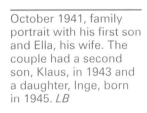

October 1941, family
portrait with his first son
and Ella, his wife. The
couple had a second
son, Klaus, in 1943 and
a daughter, Inge, born
in 1945. *LB*

On October 29 U-201 left Brest for its fifth combat patrol, in the direction of the west of Ireland. *UBA*

Elusive Convoys

On October 29, 1941, U-201 left Brest for the west of Ireland. Two days later, U-96 reported the presence of the OS 10 convoy, which had left Liverpool on October 25 for Freetown in West Africa with thirty-three cargo ships, in the middle of the North Atlantic. U-201 was too far away from the position to reach this convoy.

On November 5, Commander Schnee's U-boat joined the *Störtebecker* Wolf Pack, which was formed in the west of Spain to intercept the HG 75 convoy which had left Gibraltar on October 22. On November 7, the convoy changed direction, and the pack was sent to search for the SSL 91 convoy, which had left Freetown on October 27, but once again they had no success. The pack moved towards the middle of the North Atlantic.

On November 15, the search for the OS 11 convoy, out of Liverpool on November 7 for Freetown didn't yield any results either – the ocean seemed to be empty!

From November 17, the U-boats spread out on a line of 500 miles, between Ireland in the north and the Azores in the south, but still without success. Two days later, the U-boat Corps Command ordered its U-boats to form three distinct lines to try to locate targets; for six days U-201 was affected to the line formed by the *Gödecke* Wolf Pack. No convoys were sighted.

From November 25 to December 4, U-201 was affected to a third pack called *Letzte Ritter*, but it still didn't spot the OG 77 convoy which had left Liverpool on November 25 and which had been spotted during an air recognition three days earlier.

Empty-handed After Forty-two Days!

On December 1, nearly out of fuel, U-201 was forced to make a half-turn towards Brest which it reached on December 9, empty-handed after a forty-two-day patrol. On December 13, while it was in maintenance in the shipyards, the accidental explosion of an overloaded battery on board caused the death of two members of the crew, Seaman Machinists (*MaschOGef*) Josef Zander and Wöllner. This caused additional work on the U-boat as several compartments had been damaged, immobilizing U-201 for three and an a half months.

Four days after the Japanese attack on Pearl Harbor on December 7, 1941, Germany and Italy declared war on the United States. All restrictions concerning American ships were lifted, and Dönitz began preparing Operation "*Paukenschlag*" (Drumbeat) aimed at the coast of the United States. The German submariners present in Brest celebrated New Year's Day in the naval academy while already thinking ahead of the American coast. From then on, the entire Atlantic became a war zone. On December 31, 1941, they celebrated Commander Schnee's twenty-eighth birthday and also the Oak Leaves added to the Knight's Cross for Reinhard Suhren, Commander of the 1st Flotilla's U-564, in maintenance in Lorient since November 1. On board U-201 there were changes in personnel: Commander Schnee's Watch Officer changed.

Oberleutnant zur See Joachim Zander left the U-boat in January 1942; he took over the command of U-311 aboard which he was killed in the North Atlantic on April 22, 1944. He was replaced on U-201 by the former 3rd officer, Martin Duppel, whose vacancy was filled by a new officer, *Leutnant zur See* Eberhard Rieger, named Watch Officer 2nd watch (*IIWO*). *Obersteuermann* Karl Boddenberg, became Watch Officer 3rd watch (*IIIWO*).

U-201 leaves the U-boat base where the roofs of pen No.s 7 and 8 are nearly finished. U-83 was the first U-boat to have been taken out of the water and put in the navy base pen No.1 on September 22. This new equipment meant that the flotilla could hold more U-boats at the same time. Expansion work on the Brest U-boat base started in October 1941. The first part, nearly finished, counted two double dock pens D and E. Eight single pens, that could be drained, numbered from 1 to 8, and would soon have a total of twelve protected places. Extension work was intended to create eight supplementary spaces for the end of the summer of 1942: on the left of the existing base, three new double dock pens A, B and C are being fit out: on the right of the base are two single pens that can be drained will be built next to a separating stall and will be numbered 9 and 10. *UBA*

While surveying the ocean during the cold period of November 1941, the lookouts aboard U-201 are wearing thick padded jackets. In spite of their vigilance, they won't find any convoys this time. *LB*

To calculate the U-boat's position, the helmsman uses a sextant. *LB*

The watch continues, even during bad weather. When the lookout, after four hours of being hit by the spray, goes inside the U-boat, he will have a hard time drying out his clothes soaked with seawater. In spite of forty-two days at sea, this patrol will be unsuccessful. *LB*

In the compartment that houses the four torpedo firing tubes, crewmembers have the boring task of peeling potatoes. They wish the torpedoes could be fired so that they would have a little more room in this space where twenty-seven of them live. *LB*

On December 1, seeing that the fuel supplies are getting dangerously low, Commander Schnee gives the order everyone has been waiting for: return to the port! They arrive at the Goulet de Brest on December 9. A crown decorated with candles has been placed on the periscope. *LB*

A motorboat has just carried a bottle of cognac to U-201. *LB*

Commander Schnee opens the bottle's wrappings. *LB*

The precious liquid is passed around! *LB*

These two crewmen seem very happy to be back, perhaps they are thinking about taking a bath, which would be welcome after forty-two days at sea! *LB*

Commander Schnee directs berthing maneuvers with his megaphone. *LB*

The cognac is distributed in the "winter garden" – the platform in back of the conning tower where the 20mm anti-aircraft gun is situated. U-201 has just passed the south end of Brest Port. *LB*

U-201 berths in the
Penfeld River where the
customary welcome
committee is waiting. *LB*

On the Artillery Park
quay, a large crowd has
gathered to welcome
U-201. *LB*

The long awaited
moment after a long
patrol: a female face!

The army's brass band has set up on the pontoon. Commander Schnee savors this long awaited moment with a good cigar. *LB*

Schnee monitors the docking maneuvers. *LB*

The top of the conning tower reaches the pontoon platform. *LB*

A watch officer gives the order to stop the motors. *LB*

The army's female auxiliaries have come to welcome the crew. *LB*

Commander Schnee greets to a woman in civil dress, workers from the shipyard standing in front of the steam-crane shaft are watching them. *LB*

Hans Cohausz, chief of the 1st Flotilla, boards U-201 and salutes its commander. *LB*

The crew salutes Cohausz. *LB*

Each crewmember receives a small gift. *LB*

Cohausz gives a welcome-back speech to the crew who are lined up on the bridge. *LB*

Small presents are handed out. *LB*

Schnee thanks the female auxiliaries. *LB*

With Commander Krech (U-558) on his right, Commander Schnee embraces his friend Jürgen Oesten, former commander of U-106, who had been sent to Brest on October 20, 1941 as the new chief of the 9th U-boat Flotilla. *LB*

These two submariners have attached the pins they have just been given by two auxiliaries; the lightning bolt represents the trans-patrol units. Later some crewmembers wear them on their garrison cap as a souvenir. *LB*

Arm in arm with an auxiliary, Schnee leaves the pontoon's welcome platform to go ashore. *LB*

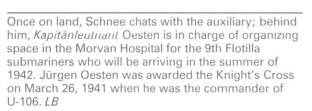

Once on land, Schnee chats with the auxiliary; behind him, *Kapitänleutnant* Oesten is in charge of organızıng space in the Morvan Hospital for the 9th Flotilla submariners who will be arriving in the summer of 1942. Jürgen Oesten was awarded the Knight's Cross on March 26, 1941 when he was the commander of U-106. *LB*

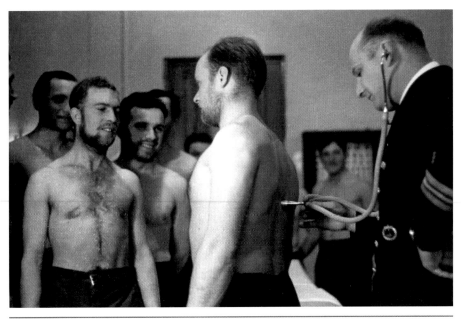

As soon as they return to shore U-201's crewmembers undergo an obligatory medical exam in the naval academy. The doctor has already been on patrols aboard a U-boat, as his decoration shows. *LB*

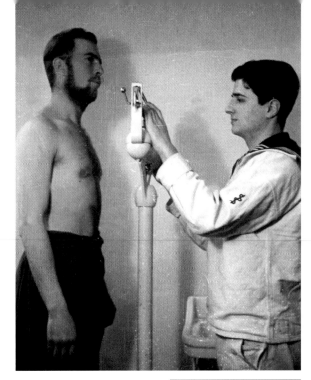

Being weighed by a medic. *LB*

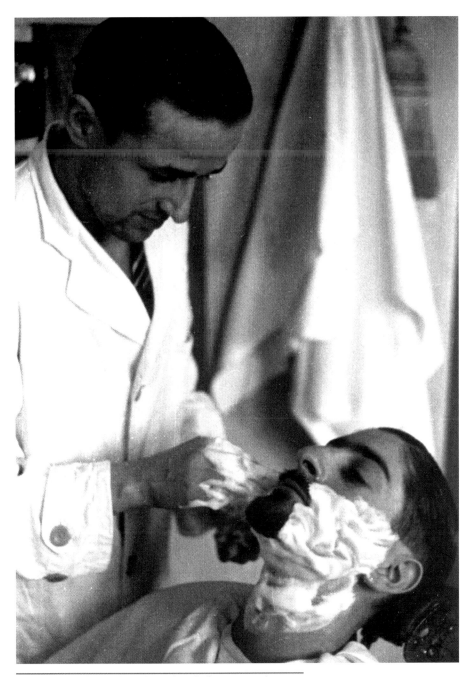

The barber trims this submariner's forty-two-day beard. *LB*

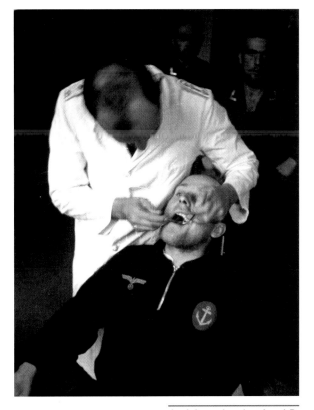

A visit to the dentist. *LB*

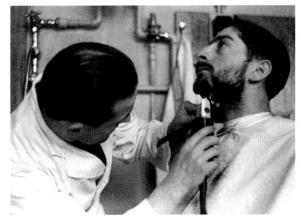

Then a close shave. *LB*

The barber's waiting room. *LB*

After a month and a half in the Atlantic, this submariner is catching up on news from the front. *LB*

Coming out from the barber, this submariner has decided to keep his goatee and moustache. *LB*

On December 11, 1941, a ceremony is held in the naval academy's Jean Bart Place for U-83's departure for the Mediterranean. The 1st Flotilla's General Staff salute the crewmembers and wish them good luck. Commander Schnee is there, in the center, to say goodbye to his comrades. This massive dispatch of U-boats to the Mediterranean in December 1941 was a great loss for the 1st Flotilla. As soon as they passed through Gibraltar they fell under the command of the 29th Flotilla based at La Spezia. The 1st Flotilla's number fell to fifteen operational U-boats on December 31, 1941. *UBA*

The photo/card Adi Schnee sent to his wife Ella for Christmas 1941. *LB*

Extensions carried out on the base in March 1942. The double dock pens A, B and C are nearly finished; the metal girders will be completely covered in cement. *LB*

On February 14, 1942, a new chief was named as the head of the 1st Flotilla to replace *Korvettenkapitän* Cohausz; *Kapitänleutnant* Heinz Buchholz had commanded two U-boats in the pre-war period before spending two years in the post of Chief of the Torpedo Service within the 24th Training Flotilla in the Baltic Sea.

On March 1, 1942, Adalbert Schnee was promoted to the rank of *Kapitänleutnant*. The same month saw the beginning of re-supplying at sea operations by supply U-boats, which meant that the VII-type U-boats could travel to the American coast. The U-201 left Brest on March 24, 1942, for Lorient for a short time. Indeed since mid-March, U-boats going to or from Brest had to pass by Lorient.

This was the result of studying the charts captured on the British destroyer *Campbeltown*, before its explosion in St. Nazaire on March 28, 1942, which showed that old sealanes to access Brest called "Sternbild" and "Rippenbruch" were mined and had to be circumvented. The mines had been placed by the British to cut the lanes of the Gulf of Gascogne in a methodical way, starting in the north, by creating minefields after the 200 meters mark.

The Lorient approach lanes from the north "*Jugend Liebe*" and "*Bogenlampe*" were also closed because of mines, so the U-boats in Brest had to use the southern access lane in Lorient called "*Cedernland*," and then follow the coast according to the "*Rosa*" line to arrive in Lorient which was used as an intermediate port in order to avoid any air danger.

During the day they remained in Lorient and in the evening they continued their journey out to sea or towards Brest. The half-day lost each time had to be accepted. This practice lasted until mid-July 1942, the time needed for the minesweepers to clear the direct access lanes to Brest.

An Argentine Ship Hit by Mistake

On March 25, U-201 left Lorient for the American coast which it reached in a little over three weeks. On April 18, at 00:46, the U-boat torpedoed the 7,417-ton Argentinean tanker *Victoria*, a neutral ship, 300 miles southeast of New York. The tanker, hit by a second torpedo at 01:45, was evacuated by its crew, but as it didn't sink they re-boarded from the three destroyers which had rescued them. Towed by the destroyer *USS Owl*, the *Victoria* and its crew returned the port in New York where the tanker was repaired.

Argentina wasn't pleased with this incident; its diplomatic representative in Germany sent a letter of protest on June 9 to the Foreign Minister Joachim von Ribbentrop to announce that such an error should not have been made, because the tanker would have sailed with all fires lit, with its Argentinean flag on the topmost mast, as well as its country's colors on its sides with the inscription in large letters "Argentinean Republic." Moreover firing the torpedoes would have taken place in full daylight.

In the German reply of June 16, the Ministry for Foreign Affairs excused itself to Argentina, and said that in his report the U-boat commander had explained that he had fired the torpedoes at the tanker not in full daylight but during the night, and that at 600 meters away it could not distinguish its nationality markings because they were not lit up. It was only after having fired its second torpedo that it saw the colors of the Argentinean flag on the side of the ship, this having been lit up during evacuation procedures. Radio exchanges with the *BdU*, ordering it to cease its attack against this neutral boat, stopped the ship from being sunk.

On March 1, 1942, Adalbert Schnee is promoted to the rank of Lieutenant Commander (*Kapitänleutnant*). *LB*

Good Hunting Along the American Coast

U-201 travelled towards Cape Hatteras, further south, where it sank the 2,027-ton Norwegian cargo ship *Breaking* on April 21, then the following day at 03:29, the 6,069-ton American cargo ship *San Jacinto* by torpedo and seventy-nine 80mm rounds, the ship was on fire when it sank a little after 3:00a.m. The same day at 09:27, U-201 took its last victim, the 7,217-ton British cargo ship *Derryheen*.

After this U-boat turned back towards France. After a one-day call in Lorient on May 20, 1942, it arrived in its homeport of Brest the following day. The result of this fifty-nine-day patrol on the American coast was three ships sunk for a tonnage of 15,313 tons and one 7,417-ton ship damaged.

At 19:30 on March 25, U-109 and U-201 leave Lorient at the same time, heading for the American coast. They will pass St. Michel Isle. *UBA*

At 09:35 on March 25, 1942, U-201, which had left Brest the day before, and U-506 coming back from a patrol in the Atlantic arrive at about the same time in Lorient. In the foreground, U-507 arrived fifteen minutes earlier. In the background, the light-cruiser *Strasbourg* in its role as a DCA. *UBA*

In his private cabin, Commander Schnee plays backgammon with a crewmember. Board games help pass the time during the three-week crossing of the Atlantic. *LB*

On the commander's cupboard doors are two portraits of crewmembers, accidently killed when batteries blew up on December 13, 1941. *LB*

In the control room, Seaman 1st Class Johannes traces the U-boat's itinerary on a sea chart. On his garrison cap he has a lightning bolt pin – a souvenir given to him by an army female transpatrol auxiliary when the U-boat was in Brest. *LB*

April 18, 1942: U-201 is 300 miles southeast of New York when an oil tanker is sighted. Boatswain's Mate Kurt Grünow is at the diving controls. *LB*

Commander Schnee watches the target through the periscope in the control room. *LB*

Boatswain's Mate Kurt Haare, at the commands of the torpedo adjustment, listens to the firing coordinates sent from the control room. *LB*

This crewmember is ready to press the button to fire a torpedo. *LB*

The target has been hit! *LB*

Obersteuermann Karl Boddenberg, chronometer in his hand, waits for the detonation. In September 1942, he left U-201 to follow a commander's training course. He took command of U-963 in February 1943. *LB*

On April 22, U-201 torpedoed the American cargo ship *San Jacinto*. The torpedo wasn't enough to sink it, so the commander ordered the job to be finished by artillery. Several crewmembers formed a chain to bring the 88mm shells up to the bridge, after they had been taken out of their waterproof storage. *LB*

The shells arriving in the conning tower via the hatch. On the left is *Obergefreiter* Ulrich Kodura. *LB*

A trap door in the conning tower is used to transfer the shells onto the bridge where the gun is. Radio Seaman (*FkOGef*) Heinz Laurin is waiting for them. *LB*

U-201's gun in action. It takes seventy-nine rounds to sink the cargo ship *San Jacinto*. *LB*

At 09:27 on April 22, the British cargo ship *Derryheen* is torpedoed in full daylight. *Oberleutnant zur See* Martin Düppel, adjusts the aim using his Uzo binoculars. He will leave U-201 in October 1942 to enter a commander's training course. He took command of U-959 in January 1943. *LB*

The cargo ship sinks. It is U-201's last victim in the seas off the American coast. *LB*

During the return journey Commander Schnee plays a tune on the accordion; in the middle of the Atlantic – the sky is obviously free of planes. *LB*

Before arriving in the port, four victory pennants, made during the return journey, are displayed on top of the periscope. *LB*

U-201 brings back four pennants: three white for cargo ships, the fourth with a red border for the oil tanker. *LB*

On May 20, 1942, U-201 is escorted to Lorient where it arrives at 09:52. *LB*

A photo of the conning tower; a souvenir of the short call in Lorient. Above is the pennant for the Argentinean oil tanker *Victoria,* damaged on April 18, plus those of the *Bris*, *San Jacinto* and *Derryheen* cargo ships sunk between April 21 and 22. *LB*

This painting refers to Commander Schnee whose name in English means "snow." *LB*

Lorient: the last touches of a painting of a snowman on the U-201 conning tower are done by *MaschOGef* Kodura and Wieckmann. *LB*

A short stop in the Scorff waiting for their departure at 21:32. Waiting for dusk means that they can reach Brest with maximum security. *LB*

A pause against the rail of the "winter garden." The barrel of the 20mm anti-aircraft gun has been dismantled. *LB*

Another member prepares a fresh salad, a luxury after a fifty-eight-day patrol! *LB*

A crewmember sends up cakes and coffee through the hatch that opens onto the conning tower from the control room. *LB*

U-201's crew watches U-701's departure for the American coast. When they arrive they will find that conditions have changed: the Americans have adopted the convoy system as the British have forcibly suggested. This U-boat was sunk by an aircraft on July 7, 1942, and thirty-nine members of the crew lost their lives. *LB*

U-67 follows U-701 to the American coast. It will have better luck in the Florida and Mexican Gulf sector; it returned to Lorient in August. *LB*

On May 21, U-201 nears Brest. Schnee plays a tune on the accordion. In the middle is *MaschMt (Diesel)* Artür Netter. *LB*

Several men use binoculars to see their welcoming committee on a pontoon on the south jetty. *LB*

A woman offers a bouquet of flowers to Schnee. *LB*

During the welcoming ceremony, U-201 is berthed in front of the U-boat base. *LB*

The U-boat base in 1942, below the naval academy requisitioned by the 1st Flotilla. *LB*

Plan of the U-boat base in Brest. *Drawing by Anthony Guychard*

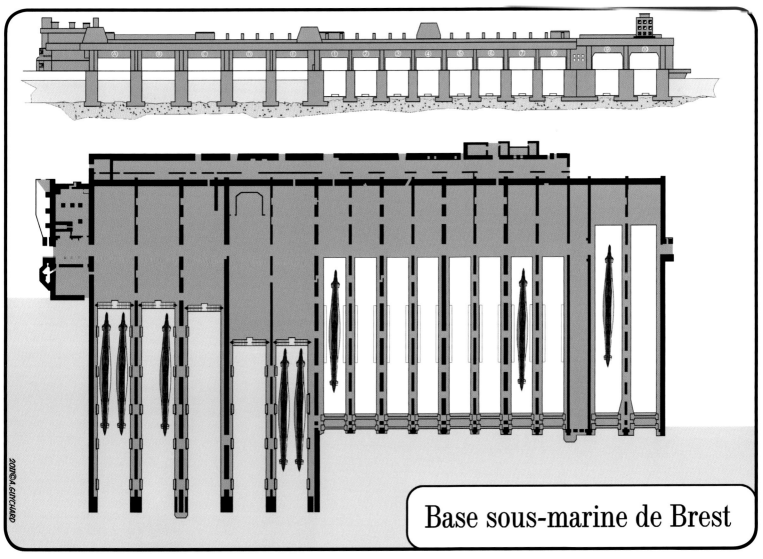

Base sous-marine de Brest

Rapid Victories

On June 27, 1942, *Kapitänleutnant* Adi Schnee, as his friends called him, left Brest for his last patrol on U-201, heading for the middle of the Atlantic. On July 3, it joined the *Hai* Wolf Pack. On July 6, it sank the 14,443-ton British cargo ship *Avila Star*, the ship having the heaviest tonnage to its credit.

On July 10, the *Hai* Wolf Pack began hunting between the twentieth and twenty-fifth meridian. The following day, the OS 33 convoy was spotted by one of the U-boats in the pack, south of the Azores. This convoy had left Liverpool on July 1 with forty ships, some of which were bound for Freetown, the rest for South America.

U-201 and U-116 took up the chase of those headed for South America. In the early hours of July 12 they fired almost simultaneously on the 7,093-ton British cargo ship *Cortona*. Damaged, it was finally sunk by a torpedo from U-201 at 00:41. A few hours later, U-201 torpedoed the 5,242-ton British cargo ship *Siris*, which sank two hours later, after being hit by 100 88mm shells from the gun on board. The following day July 13 at 02:21, U-201 torpedoed and sank the 6,723-ton British cargo ship *Sithonia*. The pursuit of this convoy stopped, it had lost six ships.

On June 27, 1942, U-201 leaves the U-boat base in Brest for its seventh combat patrol. The protection nets to stop bombs dropped from planes reaching the pens have been opened. *LB*

The Hunt Continues

U-201, still within the *Hai* Wolf Pack, continued the hunt. On July 15, it sunk the lone 6,990-ton British tanker *British Yeoman*. Once again, this torpedoed ship was sunk by artillery; sixty-one rounds were necessary. The *Hai* Wolf Pack headed south, passing between the Cape Verde Islands and the African coast.

After having passed Dakar on July 21, U-Boats left the pack, dispersing to try to find targets independently. On July 25 at 23:05, U-201 took its last victim of the patrol, a battleship this time. It was the 545-ton armed merchant trawler *HMS Laertes*, sunk by torpedo 180 miles southwest of Freetown. U-201 then turned north, towards its home base in Brest which it reached on August 8, 1942. With six ships sunk representing 41,036 tons, it was Commander Schnee's most successful patrol. It enabled him to exceed the theoretical bar of 200,000 tons of ships sunk (in reality, as a commander of U-60 and U-201, he sank twenty-four boats for 98,565 tons and damaged three others for 28,820 tons).

At the beginning of the patrol, foodstuffs are stocked all over ... even in the control room! *LB*

He therefore added the Oak Leaves to his Knight's Cross on July 15. In Brest, he was welcomed by *Kapitänleutnant* Werner Winter, appointed new chief of the 1st Flotilla on July 17, to replace Heinz Buchholz. (This latter returned to sea as the commander of U-195. He was killed on U-177 on February 6, 1944). The new flotilla chief had experience as the commander of a U-boat, on which he won the Knight's Cross, and a good knowledge of official organization, thanks to his time with the U-boat Corps General Staff from November 1939 to August 1941.

Commander Schnee with his binoculars searches for ship masts in the distance. *LB*

The forward torpedo firing tube trap-opening system. *LB*

Schnee looking through the periscope situated in the conning tower. On July 6, he sinks a large 14,443-ton British cargo ship, *Avila Star*, the heaviest ship he has sunk since taking command of U-201. *LB*

The convoy is attacked at night; a cargo ship launches a flare to help the escort ships spot U-boat conning towers on the surface. *LB*

U-201 passes the Goulet de Brest. A buoy from the British armed merchant trawler *HMS Laertes,* sunk on July 25, has been attached to the aerial as a trophy. Since mid-July, the ship lanes to this port have been completely dragged for magnetic mines, dropped by the dozens, until the departure of the flotilla for the high seas in February 1942; a passage by Lorient is no longer obligatory. *UBA*

U-201 arrives at the south pier in the large natural harbor with six pennants, returning from a patrol of a month and a half that took it to the African coast. *LB*

Kapitänleutnant Winter is saluted by the crew on the bridge. *Charita*

The conning tower has been decorated with a large oak-leaf crown brought by motor boat, in homage to Commander Schnee who had received his Oak Leaves to add to his Knight's Cross on July 15, 1942. Oak tree branches have even been wound around the periscope from which six pennants hang, representing the five merchant ships and one battleship sunk during the patrol. *UBA*

After seven patrols, Adi Schnee has become a specialist in convoy attack. Admiral Dönitz persuaded him to accept a post on land with his staff. *LB*

After a visit to Berlin to receive the Oak Leaves to add to his Knight's Cross, Schnee returns to Brest at the beginning of September to say goodbye to his crew, with whom he poses for the last time. He will be leaving Günther Rosenberg, former commander of U-351, in charge of his U-boat that leaves on operations on September 6. With the departure of Commanders Schnee and Suhren, both of whom have jobs on land, and the accidental death of Rolf Mützelburg, mortally injured when he dove off his conning tower, the 1st Flotilla lost its three most highly decorated commanders. At the end of September, the only commander decorated with the Knight's Cross to remain is Günter Krech of U-558. With the acceleration of the Battle of the Atlantic, these decorations are becoming increasingly rare in Brest. Most of the later commanders were trained as watch officers on U-boats operating during 1941, or were commanders of U-boats transformed into training boats in the Baltic Sea. The Allies' technological advances, and the tenacity of the British Navy are going to make life very difficult for them. *LB*

A souvenir postcard printed in Germany, recounting the story of Adalbert Schnee, edited for the occasion of his last decoration. *LB*

October 22, 1942, just before taking up his post with the General Staff of the U-boat corps, Adalbert Schnee visits U-201's patron city to sign the visitors' book. *LB*

War's End

To avoid any danger following the British raid on St. Nazaire during the night of March 27/28, 1942, the General Staff of the U-boat corps has been transferred from Lorient to Paris. A ceremony has been organized in front of the building they have requisitioned on Marechal Maunoury Boulevard in the 16th district of Paris. Dönitz salutes the officers of his General Staff; in front of the door are *Kapitän* Godft, head of the Operations Department and *Kapitän* Hans-Rudolf Rösing, head of U-boats for the West (*FdU-West*). *LB*

Head of Anti-convoy Operations for the General Staff of the U-boat Corps, October 1942 to February 1944

*K*apitänleutnant Adalbert Schnee was the 105th soldier in the entire German *Wehrmacht* to have received the Knight's Cross with Oak Leaves. He remained for two months at the disposal of the 1st Flotilla, which meant he could travel to Germany to receive his new decoration and where he spent part of his leave with his family. He then paid another visit to his U-boat's patron city, Remscheid. Returning to Brest, he bid farewell to his crew who would

be leaving again for two new patrols with a new commander; the U-boat was destroyed on February 17, 1943 after being boarded by the crew of a British destroyer who had forced it to re-surface using depth charges.

His results on U-201, with twenty-two ships sunk, fifteen of which were part of convoys, won him a job on land with the U-boat Corps Command, where his experience in the fight against convoys proved to be very useful. He was nominated Convoy Staff Officer (*Geleitzugs-Asto*), chief of anti-convoy operations in the Atlantic, with the U-boat Corps Command based in Paris until the end 1942 then in Germany close to Berlin. He remained in this post, close to *Großadmiral* Dönitz until February 1944, after which he spent five months with the Division of Naval Operations.

Commander of U-2511, July 1944 to May 1945

On July 24, 1944, Adalbert Schnee was appointed to supervise the finishing touches to U-2511, one of the first revolutionary XXI-type U-boats being built in the shipyards in Hamburg. On September 29, 1944, he took command of U-2511 launched the same day. He was promoted to the rank of *Korvettenkapitän* on December 1. His chief engineer was Gerd Suhren; one of the rare engineers to be decorated with the Knight's Cross and who was the brother of the highly decorated Commander Teddy Suhren.

On January 30 1945, U-2511, a 1,621-ton U-boat, left Danzig where it had been tested, with dozens of refugees on board who wanted to escape capture by the Red Army. The same day, the large German cruiser *Wilhelm Gustloff*, sailing under neutral flags and which had announced by radio that it only transported civil refugees, was torpedoed by the Soviet submarine S-13 in the Baltic Sea. Several thousand people were on board, and

Photo taken in November 1942: in an office of the General Staff of the U-boat corps in Paris and published in the first edition of *Signal* magazine in February 1943. On the left, Schnee, in the middle Dönitz who will be named Chief of the German Navy in January 1943 and promoted to the rank of *Großadmiral*, on the right *Kapitän* Godt. *LB*

about 6,000 died. Commander Schnee re-surfaced several times near the Leba delta to recover as many survivors as possible, in spite of the risk of the presence of mines, Russian ships and enemy submarines. He took the survivors to Sässnitz Port on Rügen Island.

Crew training aboard this new U-boat lasted until March 14, 1945. On March 16, U-2511 left Kiel with the 11th Combat Flotilla; it was the first XXI type in operation. It reached the Horten Base in Norway on March 23, where new crash-dive tests were carried out.

On October 26, 1942, *Kapitänleutnant* Schnee begins his new job on land, dealing with U-boat attacks on convoys. *LB*

Kapitän zur See Rösing discusses naval strategy with Adalbert Schnee at Pignerolle Chateau. The end of May 1943 sees a turn in the Battle of the Atlantic. Dönitz has ordered a temporary retreat of all U-boats from the battle area in the North Atlantic after the Allies have sunk forty U-boats during the month. *LB*

On February 12, 1943, the German magazine *Hamburger Illustrierte* published an extensive article on Commander Schnee and U-201, written by war correspondent Prokop. It was about the patrol along the American coast that he had taken part in, from March to May 1942. Only five days after the article came out, forced to surface because of depth charges, U-201 was rammed by a British destroyer and sunk with all hands lost. *LB*

Beginning of 1943: A meal at Pignerolle Chateau, headquarters of the Command of U-boats for the West. From left to right: *Oberleutnant* Ilsebeck an officer of U-boats for the West (*FdU-West*), *Kapitänleutnant* Herbert Schultze former commander of U-48 and 6th officer under the Commander-in-Chief of U-boats (*BdU*), Rosing officer of U-boats for the West (*FdU-West*), *Großadmiral* Dönitz, *Korvettenkapitän* Günter Hessler the admiral's son-in-law and 1st officer under the Commander-in-Chief of U-boats (*BdU*), Lieutenant Commander Daublebsky von Eichain 2nd officer under the Commander-in-Chief of U-boats (*BdU*) and who will be promoted to 1st officer of U-boats for the West (*FdU-West*) after February 1943, and Adalbert Schnee. March 1943 was a record for U-boats that sunk 500,000 tons of Allied ships in twenty days. *LB*

Dönitz preparing to leave Pignerolle, and Schnee getting into his car. On the chateau steps is Hans-Rudolf Rösing. *LB*

On April 3, it left Horten for Bergen which it reached on April 8, 1945. On April 30, 1945, it left the port to carry out the first true operational patrol of an XXI-type U-boat. On May 4, it had just received the cease-fire order from Dönitz sent to all U-boats when it came across a fleet of British battleships, one of which was *HMS Norfolk*! U-2511 approached to 600 meters and simulated an attack; as it wasn't detected on the battleship's Asdic System it escaped reprisals. It reached Bergen on May 5, 1945. Talking it over a few days later with officers from the *Norfolk*, they declared that it was incredible that they hadn't succeeded in detecting the U-boat!

It was his seventeenth and last combat patrol aboard a U-boat. He had been present during their evolution during the war, from the II-type to the XXI-type, covering all the Atlantic Ocean, from Norwegian waters to the African and American coasts! Loaded with 200 tons of fuel and twenty-two tons of provisions, U-2511 could have gone to Japan without stopping in a port of call!

Narvik, summer 1944: Adalbert Schnee, transferred since February to the General Staff of the Direction of Naval Operations, meets up with his friend Teddy Suhren, who since May is Chief of U-boats in Norway (*FdU-Norwegen*). Teddy Suhren became famous throughout the U-boat corps during his arrival in Brest on September 18, 1942 when he was commander of U-564. As his U-boat approached the pontoon where his comrades and all the officers were gathered to congratulate him for receiving Swords for his Knight's Cross with Oak Leaves, he grabbed his megaphone and shouted across to his friend Commander Horst Uphoff (who was known to make jokes in private about the Third Reich Government): *"Hey there! Are the Nazis still in power?"* before calling down to the engine room and ordering *"all engines astern"*! Since the Allied landings in Normandy, Teddy Suhren organized the U-boats arriving in Norway that had once been stationed in France, the flotillas of which have been dissolved. *UBA*

The insignia on the garrison cap worn aboard U-2511 represents a snowman. *LB*

On U-2511's forward bridge in May 1945: Watch Officer Lüden and on the right Reinhard König, chief engineer of U-2506, another XXI-type to arrive in Bergen. Previously, this officer mechanic was on U-123, whose former commander, Horst von Schroeter, also changed U-boats for U-2506. *UBA*

Bergen, spring 1945. On the left is U-2511 commanded by Adalbert Schnee; on the right, U-3514. Out of the 120 XXI-type U-boats in service, only twenty-six managed to reach Norway. *UBA*

The emblem painted on U-2511's conning tower is a snowman. The chief engineer on this U-boat is Gerd Suhren, Teddy Suhren's brother! *UBA*

Its batteries enabled it to reach an exceptional speed of seventeen knots underwater, enabling it to escape any surface pursuit. Out of the 120 XXI-type U-boats launched by the *Kriegsmarine* up to May 1945, only eighty-six had completely trained crews aboard. A total of twenty-six of them succeeded in reaching Norway in May, which included U-2502 (Heinz Franke) damaged on April 19 by an air attack, U-2506 (Horst von Schroeter), U-2513 (Erich Topp) and U-2518 (Friedrich Wiedner, future Roland Morillot in the French Navy, captured in Horten). But only U-2511 and U-3008 carried out actual combat patrols. The majority of the other XXI types remained in Germany and were damaged by bombardments, mainly on Hamburg, or were sabotaged by their crew in the days preceding May 8, 1945.

On the Frieleneskaien quay in Bergen: a discussion between Adi Schnee, U-861 Commander Jürgen Oesten, former U-1202 Commander Rolf Thomsen and former U-96 Commander Heinrich Lehmann-Willenbrock now chief of the 11th Flotilla in Bergen. *UBA*

Post-war

Korvettenkapitän Schnee was made a prisoner of war on May 9, 1945 in Norway. From September 1, he served over three months on a minesweeper charged with removing mines set along the German coast. Discharged from the *Kriegsmarine* on December 6 1945, he took a commercial training course and worked for several years as a representative.

He also spent a lot of time with his three children Jürgen, Klaus and Inge, born in 1941, 1943 and 1945. He became the president of the Association of Former German Submariners and organized meetings between submariners around the world. He spent a lot of time with Admiral Dönitz, until his death in December 1980, and saw a lot of the Suhren brothers as well as Ali Cremer, the former commander of U-333. But he missed the sea; from 1970 to 1980 he became the director of a sailing

Introductory letter written by Adalbert Schnee, president of the Association of Former German Submariners, at the annual meeting of the submariners of the countries in the West, that was held in Cologne in May 1967.

school on Elba Island in the Mediterranean Sea. He owned two yachts named *Elladi* I and II, taken from a part of his wife's name "Ella" and his nickname "Adi." President of the Association of U-boat Crews (*Verband DER U-Boots-Fahrer*), he died on November 4, 1982 in Hamburg.

Farewell to U-boats. Most of them, in keeping with Operation *Deadlight*, will be sunk by the British off the coast of Scotland in a loch that is 2,500 meters deep. *UBA*

Bergen, June 1945: Several officers have gathered to salute the departure of U-boats for England. From left to right: Commander Günther Pulst of U-978, Rolf Thomsen, H. Knappmann Watch Officer on U-2501, Herbert Panknin Chief Engineer on U-861, Jürgen Oesten, Adalbert Schnee, Lüden Second Watch Officer on U-2511, Reinhard König Watch Officer on U-2506, Commander Günter Lüth of U-1057, Heinrich Lehmann-Willenbrock and Gerd Suhren Chief Engineer on U-2511. *UBA*

Adalbert Schnee looking through U-995's periscope; it is the only VII-type U-boat to have survived the war. It is still in front of the Kiel-Laboe Naval Memorial. *LB*

Frohe Weihnacht

und ein glückliches Neues Jahr

WÜNSCHT DER

VERBAND DEUTSCHER U-BOOTFAHRER

A. Schnee

Christmas greetings card sent by Adalbert Schnee on behalf of the Association of Former German Submariners in 1967. *LB*

Schnee spent a lot of time with Karl Dönitz during the last years of his life up to his death in December 1980. *LB*

One of the last photos of Schnee taken on August 28, 1982 chatting with his life-long friend Teddy Suhren, who survived him by two years. *LB*

Author Luc Braeuer (*right*), at the U-Boot Archive at Cuxhaven, wishes to thank Mr. Horst Bredow († February 22, 2015), creator of the archives for the use of images in this book. *LB*

GERMAN U-BOAT ACE
Luc Braeuer

Rolf Mützelburg

The Patrols
of U-203
in World War II

German U-Boat Ace Rolf Mützelburg

The Patrols of U-203
in World War II

Luc Braeuer

German naval officer Rolf Mützelburg was one of the outstanding figures of the WWII German U-boat arm. After obtaining regular successes against the North Atlantic convoys during his first four missions, he found new victims directly along the shores of Canada. Mützelburg received the highest decorations of the period and became one of the top U-boat aces. Furthermore, he shared with Adalbert Schnee, Teddy Suhren, and Erich Topp, the rare privilege of being affectionately nicknamed by Admiral Dönitz as "The Four Aces." The discovery of a photo album from a U-203 crew member, complemented by images sourced at the U-Boat Archive at Cuxhaven, allows us to illustrate the astonishing history of this U-boat with 240 photographs and documents. The eleven combat missions of U-203 are precisely described thanks to numerous maps and sketches and the complete translation of its logbook.

Size: 9" x 12" | 240 color and b/w images | 88 pp. | ISBN: 978-0-7643-4835-8 | hard cover | $29.99

Schiffer books may be ordered from your local bookstore,
or they may be ordered directly from the publisher by writing to:
Schiffer Publishing, Ltd.
4880 Lower Valley Rd.
Atglen, PA 19310
(610) 593-1777; Fax (610) 593-2002
E-mail: Info@schifferbooks.com

Please visit our website catalog at
www.schifferbooks.com or write for a free catalog.

Printed in China